PASTORAL PITFALLS
AND HOW TO AVOID THEM

A STUDY SERIES FOR PASTORAL STUDY GROUPS

PETER C. GARRISON

C.S.S. Publishing Co., Inc.
Lima, Ohio

PASTORAL PITFALLS AND HOW TO AVOID THEM:
A Study Series for Pastoral Study Groups

Copyright © 1990 by
The C.S.S. Publishing Company, Inc.
Lima, Ohio
Reprinted 1994

All rights reserved. No part of this publication may be reproduced, stored in a retrieval system, or transmitted in any form or by any means, electronic, mechanical, photocopying, recording, or otherwise, without the prior permission of the publisher. Inquiries should be addressed to: The C.S.S. Publishing Company, Inc., 628 South Main Street, Lima, Ohio 45804.

Library of Congress Cataloging-in-Publication Data

Garrison, Peter C., 1951-
  Pastoral pitfalls and how to avoid them : a study series for pastoral support groups / Peter Garrison.
    p.   cm.
  ISBN 1-55673-208-2
  1. Pastoral theology. 2. Clergy — Office. I. Title. II. Title: Pastoral support groups.
BV4011.G35   1990
253—dc20
                                        89-29670
                                            CIP

9024 / ISBN 1-55673-208-2   PRINTED IN U.S.A.

Acknowledgments

Many thanks to my clergy cluster and their spouses for their prayers and help: Rev. Jim and Ruth Brun, Rev. Phil and Jean Gangsei, Rev. Don and Margaret Fisher, Rev. Al and Kay Cassel, and Youth Minister Mike and Karlene Harvey. Special thanks to my pastor and friend, Rev. Dr. William Bragstad and my favorite agnostic, Dr. Tom Garrison, for their suggestions and observations.

Thank you, Joanne, for your constant enthusiasm, support and love.

Dedication

To Mom and Dad

Notes

Bible quotations are from the Revised Standard Version.

Quotations from Martin Luther are from, *What Luther Says — A Practical In-Home Anthology for the Active Christian*, Concordia Publishing House, St. Louis, eighth printing 1986. ed. Ewald M. Plass. Printed with permission.

The Purpose of This Book

This book will help ministers to identify pastoral problems that, if left unresolved, will negatively effect the pastor's ministry.

Clergy usually meet weekly in small groups to discuss the text we will be preaching on the coming Sunday. Often as not, the conversation includes important but unfocused concerns about recurring problems that have historically harassed the professional minister. These problems are: being seen as some sort of good-luck charm, being put on the pedestal of undue adoration, becoming discouraged in evangelism and stewardship efforts and dealing with the presence of evil. In our personal lives, we pastors deal with the day-to-day concerns of family, housing and money along with the reality of despair, cynicism and doubt in our lives of faith.

This book focuses on and deals with these often unspoken yet continuing dilemmas of ministry. The form of the book is one which is refreshing to the professional who is subjected day-in-and-day-out to the jargon and systemic restraints of ministry.

How To Use This Book

This book may be used by individuals for meditation on and renewal of their pastoral ministries. It may be used for small group discussions, in professional retreat centers and as a practical pastoral instruction-guide in seminary classes.

Each **Pastoral Pitfall** is dealt with in a brief fictional mood piece or short story. The story deals with daily pastoral dilemmas in a dramatic, yet non-threatening manner.

A Pastor's Insight by Martin Luther or Paul deepens and broadens the dilemma to include the modern minister.

With this approach, professional ministers are free to associate their specific experiences with the mood of the story. Non-competitive opinions may then be expressed about the piece through discussion guides titled, **Questions About The Story.**

Questions About Your Ministry guides the minister to think more deeply and personally about the particular concern in regard to the minister's calling.

Questions About You guides the minister to look at his own life and lifestyle and examine them in light of God's love.

How Can Your Group Support You? calls on the clergy cluster or support group to take steps in caring for one another. When this book is used for individual study and prayer, these guides provide ideas for self-maintenance and prayerful reflection.

Meditation And Prayer Focus shares God's Word for communal and personal spiritual support.

Author's note: You will find that this book provokes lively discussions. I have found it helpful to select one person to be a facilitator for each chapter. This facilitator allows everyone to have a chance to speak and selects the questions to be addressed from the discussion guides.

Table of Contents

PITFALLS OF THE PASTORAL PERSON

1. **Letting Your Hair Down** 11
   PITFALL: When you "let your hair down" people are surprised and even hurt.

2. **The Deal** 21
   PITFALL: You have time for the ministry, but no time for yourself or your loved ones.

3. **Last Rites** 29
   PITFALL: You are tempted by death to despair of God's love for you. You seek to justify yourself.

4. **Eulogy** 37
   PITFALL: You see yourself being used by people and become bitter and cynical.

5. **The Pool** 45
   PITFALL: You become discouraged in your evangelism efforts and tire of proclaiming the Gospel.

6. **A Trick** 53
   PITFALL: You use empty faith-phrases in difficult situations, thus failing to minister to peoples' needs.

7. **In The Trenches** 61
   PITFALL: Your ministry becomes mechanical. People come to you as a dispenser of good luck.

8. **Beloved** 71
   PITFALL: Your Christian love and compassion is misunderstood as sexual seduction.

9. **The Sacrifice** 77
   PITFALL: People see worship at church as a good work that will get them to heaven.

10. **The Race For The Dead** 85
    PITFALL: You and the associate pastor compete against one another and divide the church.

– 1 –
Letting Your Hair Down

Pitfall: When you "let your hair down" people are surprised and even hurt.

Only take care lest this liberty of yours somehow become a stumbling block to the weak.
                                                1 Corinthians 8:9

The dinner has been delightful. Chocolate and coffee are being savored as dessert. The two couples sigh almost in unison and laugh contentedly.

The one man speaks to his friend the pastor, "So how goes the God business?" The man takes a heel of bread and eats it. "Ever since I left church-school I never wanted to go back to church. Just too much power-play, and not enough room for free thinkers."

"Oh, it's a lot like your sales job, I imagine," is the pastor's reply.

The salesman's wife observes, "He says sales is a combination of a pheasant hunt and a tribal dance. You have to keep beating the bushes and quartering the field to get prospects to shoot at, and then you wind up courting and wooing them and taking care of them until death-do-you-part." She laughs a pretty laugh, proud of her mate and huntsman.

The pastor smiles. "In your sales presentation I imagine you use the old sales technique of offering the buyer "features and benefits? You know, like, 'Yes, Mr. Buyer, the beautiful feature of this car is its light aluminum construction. And the benefit to you is that you can drive faster and faster on less gas.' "

"You bet," the salesman says. He pours the pastor and his wife some more coffee. "It's the basic sales job."

"Well, the 'God business,' as you call it, is like that. I sell the feature that Christ died for us, and the benefit is eternal life."

"Boy, phrases like that really take me back to church-school. I can't believe I bought that whole program, hook-line-and-sinker. Those teachers really gave me the hard sell all right. And they knew how to close a sale, too. Hellfire and brimstone! I signed on the dotted line. Then, I just gave it all up and ran for it. Never looked back. I don't even feel guilty about it anymore."

The salesman takes another piece of bread and butters it. He sips some coffee and continues, "Guilt makes the world go 'round, right, padre? Well, guilt spun me so fast I flew off into darkest empty space. And I don't feel guilty anymore." He stabs the loaf of bread with the blunt end of the butter knife.

The salesman's wife nudges him and says, "You sure talk a lot about not feeling guilty."

The pastor and his wife see that it has happened again. They are surprised. What they see happening is this: They are being seen by their friends as symbols and not as people. The pastor and pastor's wife are used to this, but what has surprised them in this instance is that these are their old friends. And the pastoral couple had gone out to dinner in hopes of letting their hair down and being themselves.

The wife has lost her sleepy contentment and is ready for anything. The pastor and wife both lean back. The pastor puts his hand in his wife's and she puts them in her lap under the table.

The salesman's eyes are fixed on the pastor's. The salesman's eyes dart down into the depths of the coffee and back up to the candlelit brightness of the pastor's gaze. "You and the church have a sales territory all softened up for you with the world's collective guilt. But I'm immune. I've been inoculated with guilt at an early age. I can now, in my maturity, ignore its threat."

The salesman stabs again at the loaf. He is surprised at being angry. He feels oddly guilty.

"I don't give a damn for guilt," he continues. "I live a good life and treat people pretty damn well. I give to charities and ignore the church, the saints and even try to ignore you sometimes." The salesman's voice is sharp and cuts the soft ease of the mumbled conversations in the dining room. A chair leg scrapes the wood floor; a head turns.

The salesman continues "What do you do with the ones who don't care, who are the most lost of the little lambs, who don't see the "features and benefits," who aren't in the market at all, who are headed out of the pasture and towards the rocky cliffs of freedom?" The wounded crust is pointed at the pastor. The bread falls to the tablecloth.

Sometimes, at a supposedly social function, when the symbolic pressure gets too much to bear, the pastor and wife leave early. This allows them to relax. This lets the crowd talk about something other than "religion" and lets the party really begin. A party can always be a success with a discussion of peoples' "faith." But a disembodied seance on "religion" just sets up the pastoral couple as totems to be worshiped, ignored or mocked. The pastor's wife sees no retreat possible here among old friends.

"So what do you do about us lost sheep?" the salesman presses.

"Baa-baa," whispers the salesman's wife. She smiles at him.

"That's not funny, honey. I'm serious."

"Not only serious, dear, but terribly, terribly guilty it seems." She touches his shoulder. "Just relax dear. You're among friends." He shrugs off her touch.

"Guilty? Okay. Let's say I'm guilty and we're among friends. Some friends. They work for the salvation of folks all week and then go out with us to relax. Our souls are expendable, it seems."

As with any admission of guilt outside the confessional or outside any mouth but a saint's, the pastor knows the focus will now shift from the guilty party to the hearer of the confession.

The salesman continues, waving the butter knife like a toy sword, "I sort of resent your cavalier attitude in regard to my eternal soul, bud. I mean it. Why does God take a night off when you two come over to our house or we all go out to dinner?"

"Honey," the wife says, "you're being a little obnoxious. These are our friends. They need to relax from their job just like you need a break from all your pressure."

The pastor has to say something. He'd rather just listen when he is being seen as a symbol. For a totem to speak is to invite misunderstanding.

The pastor leans over the sputtering candle on the table. It's red and casts upside-down shadows up his face. "Listen," he says. "Here's the sales pitch: Come to church tomorrow. Come for a free demonstration of God's love in Jesus. Find your long-lost guilt and God's forgiveness in one convenient location."

The salesman leans forward over the candle too. "No sale, bud. I tried your model once. I've got buyer's remorse. I got kicked once and there's no education in the second kick of a mule."

"Shall I bring in the 'closer?' The Big Guy who will close the deal?"

"Who you gonna get, an angel? Jesus? Let's see him!"

The pastor takes a melodramatic breath and blows out the candle. While their eyes adjust in the dark restaurant, it seems all the light in the world is gone. Smoke rises from the candle. The pastor says, "How about Death for a heavy closer?"

"That old boogie man? I just have to keep saying "No," and like any salesman he'll have to go away eventually."

"Or you will go away," says the pastor.

"Ooooh, I'm scared now. I'm really shaking. Whether death goes or I go, either way it's the same. He'll leave me alone."

"Ah," says the pastor, "But that's the good news. You don't have to be alone. You can be with a loving God forever. Features and benefits, remember?"

"Nice try, bud. If guilt doesn't work, try fear, huh? Terror inside your soul and outside on your skin. That's a heck of a sales tool you've got."

"Well," he answers, "You just accused me of not really caring for you." The pastor leans back and smiles. "Fear and terror are just my ways of letting you know I really care."

The couples laugh as the salesman, too, leans back and smiles. A waiter comes over and clears the table, pours the last of the coffee into the couples' cups.

The pastor continues, "You see, that's another benefit of the faith. The feature is that guilt is aroused when the law condemns us all of our sin and requires our death. The benefit is that we are forgiven through the faith that is given us. What's nice is that this Gospel package is easy to market and sell because price is not a factor — Jesus picked up the tab; faith is free."

The couples are silent. They watch the waiter work.

The waiter finishes his detailed sprucing up of their table. The care with which he works might be a hint that he wants to go home. He brushes the tablecloth with a special brush. The crumbs pop up into the candlelight like tiny fireworks.

"That's it?" asks the salesman. "No big close? No dotted line to sign on?" He stands up. "I'm afraid your poor little lost sheep is still out in the dark somewhere."

They all stand up and stretch, pushing their chairs back and putting on coats.

The pastor says, "Oh, you haven't strayed as far as you suppose, little lamb. I think you've just been walking in circles, never really too far from the shepherd." He doesn't look at his salesman friend as he says, "Come to church and get your bearings again."

The salesman puts his arm around his friend the pastor. "Ha!" he laughs loudly. "I got you to work on your night off! I guess I'm not just cheap entertainment after all."

Study and Reflection Guides For: Letting One's Hair Down

The Pastoral Pitfall: When you let your hair down, people are surprised and even hurt.

A Pastor's Insight: "It behooves a prudent minister of God to preserve honor and reverence for his ministry . . . Ministers who by a stupid condescension are indiscriminately familiar and chummy . . . create contempt by their familiarity."
                                                                    Martin Luther

Questions About the Story

1. How is the pastor's vocation like a sales job?
2. How is evangelizing different than selling?
3. Do guilt and fear make the world go around?
4. Why can people talk more readily about religion than faith?
5. Is the salesman angry at God, his pastor friend, or the church?
6. Is the salesman really angry or does he feel abandoned somehow?
7. How does the pastor end up working on his night off?

Questions About Your Ministry

1. What do you think are the features of Christianity? Of the gospel of Christ? Of church? Of your ministry?
2. What are the benefits of these things?
3. How do you prospect for new sales territories, or find new people to evangelize?
4. How do you close the deal with visitors or new members?
5. How do you follow up to make sure they are being served by your ministry?

Questions About You

1. What sold you on Christianity?
2. What keeps you a loyal customer?
3. With whom do you let down your hair? Why is this important for ministers?
4. Are you very different among these friends than among people to whom you minister? Why might this be a symptom of some identity or ministry crisis?
5. Do people put higher standards for ethical and moral living on you than on themselves? Is this fair? What can you say or do about it?
6. What happens when you go to a party or social event and people discover you're a minister? What happens to you?
7. How have you been embarrassed when you've let your hair down among friends?
8. Have you ever suddenly ended up ministering to someone at a so-called social event? What happened?

How Can Your Group Support You?

1. Do you let your hair down in this group?
2. Are there any hints of competitiveness in your group?
3. Do you presume that confidentiality will be maintained?
4. Would it help to make some verbal agreements now in your group concerning letting one's hair down?

Meditation and Prayer Focus
(Luke 9:58)

1. It was lonely at the top for Jesus; uncomfortable and nowhere could he put down roots. How is your ministry like his?
2. Jesus let his followers know just how rough discipleship is. How does your selling of the gospel candy-coat this message of hardship and suffering, loneliness and service?

3. When and how does your evangelism tell it like it is?
4. How can Jesus' compassion give you comfort in your loneliness and discomfort?
5. For your closing prayers, think of times you have been lonely, feeling abandoned and uncomfortable. Ask Jesus to heal those memories and to empower you to continue in your ministry to others who are feeling lonely, abandoned and who suffer discomfort.

– 2 –
The Deal

Pitfall: You have time for the ministry,
   but no time for yourself
   or your loved ones.

Nec tecum vivere possum nec sine te. *I can live neither with you nor without you. Therefore one must diligently pray for constancy in love. It is the highest grace of God when love continues to flourish in married life.*
                                       Martin Luther

I, as a cat, have a good sense of time. I like to live in a dependable household with dependable people who come and go at set times. I, as a cat, like set obligations of availability: You pat me, I purr. You feed me, I remain truly yours. It's the deal.

The contractual agreement should work thus: They come home at certain times, I meet them, make friendly noises, roll around on the floor, seem pleased and welcoming. In return for this restrained but dependable enthusiasm on my part, they pat me and talk to me as if I understand every blessed word they say. We all appear a bit foolish, but as in any good contract one gives a bit more than one wishes and gets a bit more than one really deserves.

Lately though, the contract has broken down. They are not happy. They come and go at odd hours. They avoid one another. I cannot keep up with their coming and going and it makes me nervous.

"Where are you going now?" one will ask.

"The Olsen's cat died. They need me to go with them to the Humane Society," is the reply.

"Oh, for heaven's sake, you're a minister, not a pet mortician. Don't they have a friend to go with them?"

"They said they need me." The minister drags a sweater out of the closet. The sweater sleeve sweeps along the floor past my nose. I want to pounce on it, but I sense now is not a good time. "I have to run — don't wait up!" The sweater sleeve sweeps along the floor and out the door.

"Damn," the word reaches the crack in the door just before it closes. "Another cold meal alone. Another cold night alone."

I am sad to hear of the death of another cat. I am sad to hear that the meal will be cold, because the scraps I glean will not be fresh. I am sad, indeed.

We all used to be dependably happy. But the couple has problems. One of them is a preacher. The other is a spouse. Their marital problems are way beyond yelling, "Practice what you preach, you big phoney!" Or mumbling so only kitty ears can hear, "If you would pay as much attention to the faith as you do to your work and tennis lessons, our marriage might have a chance."

Not much preaching is heard at home anymore. Oh, it used to be. "Yak, yak, yak," with pontifications aplenty; an infallible opinion with God to back it up like some bully on a playground; the spouse reduced to a heretic smouldering with resentment, about to burst into violent flame.

I've heard the spouse say, "There's no reaching you anymore. You think you've got all the answers. Why don't you listen to me? You used to like my opinions. You don't even hear me any more. You just tune me out."

"I'm sorry, honey. I just need to relax. The parish used to be so dependable. Lately it's been frantic. I make myself so available to the people and still things just keep snowballing. I attend every meeting, every class, every outing, every prayer group and still I don't feel in control." The minister sighs.

"Then I get home to you and the kids and I just don't want to hear anymore words. I can't even be alone and quiet and relax anymore. I start thinking of the parish, or the people, or the service next Sunday or the things I've seen and heard today. The only way I can relax is to listen to the static between channels on the radio so I won't listen to the talk in my head."

Oh, it's bad all right. They're beyond trying to practice what they preach. Luckily for me, as a cat, I can practice the art of selective attention. The stereo can be on, a kid may be running near my tail, the preacher and spouse might be shouting it out over a hurried meal stuck in their throats, and I won't pay a bit of attention to any of it. But mention my name and I'm alert and ready for food or a pat. I'll purr in a dependable way and comfort them with attention and a warm-furry empathy. I'll roll over and play their game and they'll be thankful. That's the deal.

The spouse says, "All a person at church has to do is look at you in some pitiful way and call your magic name, 'Pastor' and you run to them. You're on a pretty short leash if you ask me. You've got time for everything and everyone else," the spouse continues. "You've got the warm shoulder, the cool head, the listening ear for everyone else but me, but us." A big aluminum pan is shaken in emphasis like a silver halo appearing behind the spouse's head. "We need you at home!" The halo comes down with a clang on the kitchen counter.

"But the flock needs its shepherd! Honestly, honey, they really are like little lambs; trotting over a cliff or wagging their fluffy tails while the wolves lurk nearby."

The spouse says, "I don't understand how Christ's church could have survived this long without you." Her eyebrow is raised up and her mouth smirking down. The pastor doesn't notice.

"Oh, it's not that so much as it is the gratitude in peoples' faces. They are so thankful, so needful, so ready to be helped. I've just been wearing myself out ministering to them, that's all."

The spouse sighs. "I'm tired too, you know. I have a lot to do too, you know. I have to work with people at my job. I have to take care of our family's schedule. I get tired of listening to all the family's complaints." The spouse sighs and continues.

"In fact, I'm also getting tired of all the sweet advice the church gives me. 'Well,' they'll say oh-so-helpfully, 'The other preacher and spouse did the parsonage garden this way,' or, 'The other preacher and spouse sang duets together every Sunday.'"

"They mean well," the preacher says.

"They're blood suckers."

It's about now in their arguments that I usually see the preacher's shoes move backwards to the television room. When they fight it is usually the spouse who gets in the last lick. Something like, "You drive me nuts! The church drives me nuts! And I'm not so sure that God doesn't drive me nuts."

When these arguments occur, it is important to pick, not the winner, but the loser so as to be there for them in their misery — to be ready with a purr and lick — that's the deal: to appear as a heroic confidant, to receive praise and pats.

Picking my options quickly, I see the preacher is the most approachable by being the most guilt-ridden, the most self-pitying; an easy mark for shared sympathy, and thus an easy mark for a hand-out of kitty crunchies or a pat.

Through the memories of the smells and sights and sounds of past fights, I pad over the rug after the retreating preacher. A kid runs up smiling a ritual tribal smile and is ignored in our quick march to the den of quietude. There, surrounded by the television, some fiction, and the stereo, we can practice our selective attention. We can nap or pretend to nap — a holy state akin to meditation.

As I said before, I have my wonderful sense of selective attention. I can filter out all noise by my name. When my name is called, I'm ready for food or a pat. The preacher too seems able to filter out all but the call to be a confidant, a helper, a friend, a rescuer, a judge, a slave. We each have deals to honor.

We can relax until we are called upon to honor our deal. We can nap and dream of running after a mouse or running to the rescue; of being praised and patted and purring. And, in our napping, we can be comforted that it was a dream, just a dream, should a nightmare bring to us the terror of being chased.

Study and Reflection Guides For: The Deal

Pastoral Pitfall: You spend so much time responding to the needs of your ministry, that you are too exhausted to minister to your spouse, family or yourself. You become enslaved to the ministry and, at the same time, find most of your ego-gratification there.

A Pastor's Insight: "The world says of marriage: A short joy and a long displeasure. But let it say whatever it please. Whatever God has created and wants is bound to be a mockery to it . . . To be married and to understand married life finds in it delight, love, and joy without ceasing, as Solomon says: "Whoso findeth a wife findeth a good thing" (Proverbs 18:22). These are the people who understand, who firmly believe that God has instituted marriage and joined man and woman together."

Martin Luther

Questions About the Story

1. How is the pastor's deal like the cat's?
2. What are some similar benefits?
3. What are some similar drawbacks to these deals?
4. Do you think the pastor is ministering to people or does he seem used by people? What's the difference?
5. How can the pastor better minister to:
   a. Self?
   b. Family and spouse?
   c. Parish?
   d. What does the spouse need?
   e. What can the spouse do?
   f. How can the spouse be helped?

Questions About Your Ministry

1. How many hours do you spend at work?
   a. During the day?
   b. During the night?
   c. How many emergencies do you respond to per month?
   d. How many emergencies specifically needed your pastoral presence?
   e. What is your spouse's role/identity in regard to your work?
2. Do you keep regular office hours that are well publicized? Would this cut down on the emergencies?
3. Do people know what you do in your ministry?
4. Do you consider it unprofessional to tell them what you do with your time? Why or why not? Do they have a right to know?
5. How many hours a week do you spend listening to people in your ministry? How much time listening to family?

Questions About You

1. Can the church survive without you?
2. What exactly would not get done if you didn't push it?
3. How often do you ask someone to help you with your ministry tasks?
4. How often do you ask someone to help you at home?
5. Can your marriage and/or family survive without you?
6. What is your idea of spending quality time at home?
7. How does your spouse cope with tension in his/her role?

How Can Your Group Support You?

1. Have any members of your group gone on a Christian marriage encounter? What was it like? Do they recommend such a retreat? Do your spouses have a support group?

2. Does your group have practical time management ideas for ministry and married life? Office hours? Daily plans?
3. Can anyone recommend some classes or readings for improving your time management, administration habits or communication skills?
4. Can anyone rcommend ways of politely saying, "No"?
5. Try role-playing.

Meditation and Prayer Focus

"Witness faithfully in word and deed to all people. Give and receive comfort as you serve within the church. And be of good courage, for God has called you, and your labor in the Lord is not in vain."
[*Occasional Services*, "Ordination", p. 197. © 1982 Association of Evangelical Lutheran Churches, et.al.]

1. All people includes your family. How do you witness faithfully to them?
2. How do you receive comfort as you serve within the church?
3. What comfort do you give at the church that would be missed if you didn't provide it? How about at home?
4. Under what circumstances does your courage fail?
5. How does your call strengthen your courage?
6. For your closing prayers, give thanks for times when God refreshed you when you felt your labor was in vain. Give thanks for your family, friends, support group, and church as you recall how you were refreshed to continue in your ministry to them. Ask God for continued strength.

— 3 —
Last Rites

Pitfall: You are tempted by death
to despair of God's love for you.
You seek to justify youself.

"The good angels bring terror . . . they come with a certain majesty . . . but an evil angel creeps along smoothly like a serpent . . ."

Martin Luther

One might suppose the angelic appearance at the dying pastor's bedside a welcome miracle, a confirmation of the pastor's life-long faith. Actually, the pastor considered the angel an unwelcome nuisance.

The pastor had been rehearsing some elegant and faithful last words. He had been in the process of dying for some time and had envisioned his demise as including a heroic last gasp to be long remembered by his family, friends and parish, and the bishop who had never taken him very seriously.

The angel stood over him. The angelic wings fluttering near his head created a draft where the bedcovers weren't tucked in around his neck. The pastor waved his hands above him, trying to shoo the angel away. The angel, expecting a deathbed summons, mistook the waving away for a "come hither" and sat on the bed.

"Yes?" whispered the angelic voice.

The pastor's eyes were heavy from their struggle with Morpheus. He gazed sleepily at the angel. His eyes grew a bit wider as he spoke. "The bed springs squeaked," he said.

"What?" the angel said. "What did you say about bed springs?" The angel leaned closer.

"They squeaked. I never thought about whether angels weighed anything. I guess you do if the bed squeaked when you sat down."

"You're just imagining things — me. I'm really your doubt hanging around your deathbed. I'm just another disappointment in your long life of little disappointments."

The pastor moaned a little moan. "I thought your presence here was too good to be true." The pastor moaned again. He kept wagging a bare toe from under the bedsheet. He was in pain and the odd wagging for some reason helped the pain.

The angel smiled. "Oh, I'm true enough. I just may not be who you think I am."

The pastor weakly waved a hand above him as if shooing a fly. "Do disappear, please." His hand sank like a ballerina dancing the dying swan in Swan Lake. His foot continued wagging as he spoke.

"It's confusing. Thanks for coming. I'm pretty tired." He turned his head to the wall. The pastor crossed his weakened eyes to focus on scratches and stains on the plaster. The scratches and stains moved as if caught in some tidal flow along the wall.

"You're going to die soon," the angel said. The angel was leaning over him, still seated on the bedside.

The pastor squirmed. "Your weight makes me hurt when the bed tilts. Get up. Stand up. Hover." The pastor turned from the wall onto his back. The ceiling seemed closer than before. "I know I'm going to die soon. Maybe today."

"What will be your last words, do you think?" the angel asked. "Surely not something trite."

"What might you consider trite?" The pastor panted from the effort of speaking.

"Oh, something scriptural: 'Lord Jesus, receive my spirit.' That's pretty sappy. It's so passive."

"Oh," the pastor sighed, "I was planning on using that. How about something more active, like St. Stephen's, 'Look

... I see heaven open and the Son of Man standing at the right hand of God'?"

"Well, you could use that, I suppose. But," the angel observed, "you couldn't just make those things up and lead people on. You weren't pretending all this time in your ministry, were you?"

"Sorry, I wasn't thinking. It's the morphine."

"Ah," said the angel. "The real opiate of the people. Like the faith, it makes one content and unthinking, uncritical and complacently compliant to oppression."

"A Marxist angel? I'm dying and God sends me an angel who's a Marxian dialectical social critic?" This long sentence took a lot of strength from the pastor. Still, he chuckled and winced and chuckled again. The pastor knew with whom he was dealing and was going to go out showing good form.

The angel pulled up a wheelchair and sat down. "You're confused as to the message I bear and on whose behalf I bear it." A small smirk creased the angelic face.

"I think," the pastor said, "that your smirk just gave you away. I don't think angels smirk." Over the hospital paging system a doctor's voice was being repeated and repeated. The name washed through the pastor's mind like the tide of opiate moving behind his eyes, moving the walls like seaweed.

The angel was rolling back and forth in the wheelchair. It squeaked in the pastor's ears, tormenting him in its shrillness as the wheelchair's motion made him seasick. "You see, pastor, you will soon die. And I'm here to ask you if you really believed all the stuff you preached. Think of your dreary life. Of the petty parish arguments and debates. Of the sad lonely lives and desperate deaths, the hypocrisy, the boring meetings, the way people ignored you or laughed at you and your hopes."

Memories of long nights, hard cold metal chairs, stale coffee, sad living rooms and empty pews filled the pastor's mind. He felt accused of being ineffective. Or worse, unfaithful. He wanted to blame someone else. But, as a spiritual soldier well-trained, he jumped on the blame and covered it with his own body like a soldier jumping on a grenade to save his patrol. The pastor held the blame to himself where it was safe and would do no more harm than to blow him to pieces.

The angel continued, "Now you're to be one of those lonely deaths. After all this time, where is your church, your bishop, your church council? And your family? I'll tell you where they are. They're down the hall at the vending machine deciding whether to buy a candy bar or a can of diet soda."

"I meant to be faithful. My Lord told me to be faithful. I wonder if that's the same as being effective? I suppose not. But still, I must have done some good."

"Oh, no doubt you ushered some into a peaceful death. You helped others cope with death. You helped others live a life that was smoothed over with platitudes and happy-talk," the angel said.

"No. I was with people in their ups and downs. Our Lord suffered and died. His people suffer and die. He helps us in our suffering and dying."

"You mean he helps you suffer and die? A virus does that much! Some God. Some deal! I guess once you die you'll be with your dead God," the angel sneered. The page system called out the doctor's name again and again. Nurses were suddenly between the pastor and the angel. It was cold without the bedcovers. Nurses pushed him and rolled him this way and that on the squeaking bed. It was hard for the pastor to catch his breath enough to speak.

"For an angel you don't understand much. Jesus took away death, not dying. And it wasn't that I didn't doubt or fail or find myself a hypocrite now and then — I did . . ."

"But," the angel interrupted mockingly, "what is important to your eternal salvation is that you believe in your risen Lord and he gave you this same faith so that you will live with him forever." The angel stood up from the wheelchair. "La-de-da!"

The angel reached for him. "Take my hand and I will show you something more powerful than mere trust. I will show you something you can know for sure. I will show you death. A complete death without the bother of hope."

The pastor was getting too weak to keep his eyes open. "Worship God and love your neighbor . . ." he whispered.

"You're on the way out for sure now. You're reciting formulas of faith. Take my hand. *Do something* for once! Don't just passively receive a blessing. Take a blessing by force. Don't just lie there like a lump of clay!"

The nurses were weaving a net of wires and tubes around the pastor like spiders enveloping their prey.

"That's how we started," the pastor said. "Clay in our creator's hand. Passive, full of potential through his creation . . . created in his image, bestowed with his love and righteousness for life eternal." The pastor mumbled on for a moment and was still.

The doctor ran into the room. More footsteps were running down the hall behind him. The doctor felt the cool clay of the pastor's skin. The doctor saw patients die from the outside in; getting cold first in the arms and legs, then the torso and finally the eyes become chilled and hazily congealed. The pastor's eyes were still, gazing to the side of the bed.

The pastor's family ran in. "He's gone," the doctor said. He wanted to pull the sheet over the pastor's face, but the sheet was tangled in tubes and wires. The family edged him out of the way and stood looking down at the dead pastor.

"Did he say anything, doctor? What were his last words?"

The doctor heard his voice paged; "Doctor Stephano to intensive care. Doctor Stephano to intensive care." He would have to run back down the echoing hall and up the stairway he'd just descended.

The doctor replied, "I thought I heard the pastor say, 'Lord Jesus, receive my spirit.' Then he just fell asleep." The family stood there. One held a candy bar, one held a bright aluminum can in which soda hissed. "Excuse me," the doctor said. "I have to run. I'm sorry."

The doctor ran down the hallway, past nurses and medical carts, past wheelchairs and one patient wrapped in a white sheet who floated along like a sad angel. The doctor thought, "At least that's what I thought he said. I got there too late. Anyway, it was something a pastor would say." The running doctor pushed open the stairway door and bolted heavenwards to intensive care.

Study and Reflection Guide For: Last Rites

The Pastoral Pitfall: Being tempted by death to despair of God's love for you in Christ. You seek to justify yourself.

A Pastor's Insight: "The temptation which assails faith itself is the greatest of temptations, for faith is to conquer all the other temptations and calamities. If, then, faith gives way to temptations, all the others, even the smallest overwhelm a man. But if faith remains, we can despise the severest calamities... In every temptation simply close your eyes, and follow the word."

Martin Luther

Questions About the Story

1. The pastor is accused of being trite, pretending and being ineffective in his ministry. Upon what or whom does he finally rely? Was he trite, pretending or ineffective in his faith-filled last words?
2. Who ended up saying some typical last words a pastor would say? Why these words?
3. How else did the messenger tempt or torment the pastor?

Questions About Your Ministry

1. Do you have an effective ministry? How do you know?
2. Do you have a faithful ministry? How do you know?

Questions About You

1. What do you really think about the presence of a suffering and a loving God? Is death a motivator for faith? For your faith?
2. What phrases do you find yourself using in times of trouble or worry? Are these types of prayer? Do you say them tritely or with conviction?
3. What do you want as your epitaph?
4. What would you like your last word to be?
5. Who would you want to hear or read your last words?

How Can Your Group Help You?

1. Talk about some doubts you have.
2. Talk about doubt as a part of the faith-process in worshiping our living God.
3. Share some prayer patterns that have helped you through times of doubt.
4. Have you ever seen faith as something trite or simple-minded? Share with the group what you consider trite in the faith.
5. What Bible verses do you recall that show the struggle of a Christian or even Christ struggling with doubt?
6. Talk about ways in which our risen Lord can be empathetic about our temptations and doubt. How does he strengthen our faith?

Meditation and Prayer Focus
(1 Peter 5:6-11)

1. Suffering and anxiety are part of life. How do you cast your anxieties on your God who cares for you? What do you say? What do you do?
2. What anxieties can't you seem to cast upon God?

3. What sufferings do you have today? Have you cast them upon your God who cares for you? What do you think will happen under the mighty hand of God?
4. Can you help someone in your group who has anxieties and suffering, who is tempted by the roaring lion?
5. How do you see yourself restored, established and strengthened in this life lived in Christ? In the next life?
6. What can your group do for you to help you be restored, established and strengthened in the ways you imagined?
7. How can you help them humbly under God's mighty hand?

— 4 —
Eulogy

Pitfall: You see yourself being used by
people and, as a result,
become bitter and cynical.

But Jesus said to him, "Follow me, and leave the dead to bury their own dead."
Matthew 8:22

It was an irritating mist that fell from the low clouds. I couldn't decide what shoes to wear. Would the cemetery grass be wet or merely damp? I decided to put on my old black shoes in case it had rained harder on the other side of town where the cemetery was. I didn't want to wear my new shoes to the funeral if the grass was soaked and muddy.

I gathered up my robes and cross from the sacristy, zipped them into their plastic shroud, and drove over to the funeral home. The mist built slowly on the windshield as I drove. Too little wiper action and I couldn't see where I was driving. Too much and the rubber blades would squeak across the windshield. It was an irritating mist.

It was an irritating death. The dying itself was prolonged in its agony and cost. The mourners were not regular church members and came with their tails between their legs sniffing around for some psychological closure to their suffering. I saw myself as the Christian they would throw to their fear of death; the fear that prowled and growled around them.

Funerals are often lewd festivals of self-pity. Not pity for the dead. Not celebration for the eternal life given to us through

Christ. Just a psychological closure. A nice going away party, a so-long salute to a fallen comrade so that the surviving combatants can get on with their way on life. As a Christian among the secular religious, I was a Valium, a pastoral placebo everyone knew could not stop death, only buffer the collective conscience against this bump in life's lovely lane.

I was in a self-pitying mood too. Blame it on the mist.

I walked into the funeral home. The young owner in a tuxedo said, "Your party is this way," and ushered me, as if he were a maitre d', into the parlor of mourners feasting on their grief.

"Oh, pastor," said the widow, "I'm so glad you're here." She spun me over to a corner and pointed to an ancient woman in a wheelchair. "This is Buddy's Aunt Lucille." (Buddy was over in the corner in the coffin.)

Aunt Lucille held out a thin blue and brown hand that was softly turned into a curve by arthritis. "Aunt Lucille, this is our pastor, he will help you."

I shook her hand that was as cool as wood and wondered when I had become their shepherd when they were content to be on their own, gamboling hither and yon; baa-baaing only when threatened by wolves or stuck in a gully. "Good afternoon, nice to meet you," I said, getting into the room's oddly festive atmosphere of gloom.

The widow tugged me over to some flowers that gave off a thick perfume. "Aren't these beautiful? They're from some relatives I haven't heard from in ages. Amazing how death just pulls a family together from little scattered pieces, isn't it?" Her clear blue eyes looked out from a fifty-year-old face that had no wrinkles. By pure force of will and modern medical technology, decay and death would leave no inroads on her skin. At the last trumpet, she would arise young in her timelessness. Except, I thought, resurrection doesn't concern skin and fingernails and swatches of hair, but our recongizable form: our — "selves." But why ruin her angelic plans with exegetical exactitudes?

A thin brother came over. He was dressed in black and had on black tennis shoes and a black bowtie on a black shirt.

He pulled me to another corner and leaned closely. He secreted me an envelope and said, "This is for you. I know the funeral home is supposed to do this, but I wanted to do it personally. I really appreciate your doing this — sending my brother to heaven and everything."

My mouth opened in surprise. I shut it. I opened it again and said, "God's will is that all be saved. He sent his Son because he loves his whole creation. This, of course, included your brother. You too." I throw him this gospel-truth like a lifeguard throwing a buoy to a swimmer drowning beyond his reach.

The thin brother whispered in a tone appropriate to a funeral parlor with yellow velvet wallpaper and dusty glass chandeliers, "I put something extra in there for you. I know my brother never went to church. He couldn't believe all that stuff. But I want you to say some nice words about him. For his wife and auntie, you know."

I replied with a whispered outburst, "My focus will be on Christ's promise of life eternal through the faith he so lovingly gives us! If you would like to say some nice words, a eulogy, please feel free. But I'm not going to be a toastmaster to Buddy's bon voyage." I was getting a headache.

The thin brother leaned like a bent reed against me. Punch was being served with merry little splashes across the room. He said, "Listen, you just tell them the fairy tale. You just make today a pretty ribbon tied on Buddy's life like the flowers on his coffin. But you better say something nice about my brother because he never had it good in life. And I kinda hold your God responsible for his miserable life and painful death."

He was poking his finger into the cross on my chest, backing me up against the wall. He continued in a hoarse whisper, "So you just tell them what a Good Christian he was. It'll help him and them. And it will make your God look good, too. Because right now, with Buddy in a box over there in the corner, your God looks pretty useless!" His nostrils were flared and his ears were red. I marveled at his ability to whisper with such vehemence.

The funeral director and the widow approached us, not sensing any tension. "The service can begin any time, Reverend," he said, smiling. The widow nodded.

I was tempted to say, "Let the dead bury their own dead," and walk out. Instead, I walked to the casket and closed the cover over Buddy's surprising face. (Someone had implored the embalmer to, "make him look happy to be with us one last time.") The focus was now shifted from the open display of death to the open proclaiming of life-after-death through Christ. At least, that was my plan.

Halfway through the prayers and Bible readings, the thin brother solemnly stood and came to the podium near the casket. He said, "I'd like to say some things about Buddy." I was elbowed aside and took a decorative stance near the flowers, wreaths and other funeral festoons.

The brother spoke of his love for Buddy. Of Buddy's love for his family. Of the family's love for him. Of Buddy's love of motorcycles and imported beer. Of Buddy's love of country music and the love that was on Buddy's face when he ran with his wife down the perilous rice-covered steps at the Reno city hall.

The eulogy ended when the thin brother ran out of things to say. I asked the people to stand and pray the Lord's prayer. They started out well, but their poorly reinforced memories failed along the way and I finished the prayer alone.

The mourners filed past the reopened casket to "Say goodbye one last time." We drove to the cemetery. My shoes squished in the mud. The pallbearers slipped. Nearby, an idle bulldozer grunted, anxious to fill in the hole.

Prayers were again prayed. Scripture was again read. People looked ready to go. Dirt was tossed.

As I shook hands a last time, the widow came up to me. "You know," she said, "I didn't get anything out of the service until Buddy's brother stood up and said all those nice things about Buddy. Your sermon didn't let me cry." The mist was on her lashes and she blinked the mist onto her cheek like the perfect glutinous tears in movies. "Your good news about God is just too good to believe. It didn't do anything for me. Thanks just the same. You gave a good talk."

She turned to leave and lost a high-heel in the muddy grass. She took off the other shoe and walked back barefooted through the cold grass to the hearse.

I drove home. The mist had some weight to it now. The wipers slapped back and forth. I put my robes away. As I walked into my office the associate pastor called out from her office, "How was the funeral?"

"Bad," I said. "The dead are still quite dead."

"Who's that, you or them?"

"It's hard to tell sometimes," I said. "Hard to tell."

Study and Reflection Guides For: Eulogy

The Pastoral Pitfall: Cynicism. Failing to see the good God is working in everything for those who love him. (Romans 8:28) You see yourself being used by people and become embittered.

A Pastor's Insight: "I know (says Christ) that the devil will assail you severely for My sake, to make you sad, weary, and impatient so that you stop your work and say: I wish I had never begun this . . . But (says Christ) not so! Do not let the devil, the world, or your own flesh overpower you; but think how I have loved you and still love you and how much I have spent on you that you might be righteous and saved through Me."

Martin Luther

Questions About the Story

1. The thin brother is described as a "bent reed" (Matthew 12:20). How does the pastor minister to him?
2. What might the pastor have said to the widow to minister to her at the graveside?
3. Why do you think Jesus said what he did in Matthew 8:22?
4. When in the story did you feel the pastor was being prophetic? Pastoral? Rude?
5. Who are the dead in this story? Buddy? The mourners? The pastor? His faith and ministry?

Questions About Your Ministry

1. What ministries do you do that may be considered part of a civic or secular affair? Marriage counseling? Presiding at marriage ceremonies? Chaplain at civic service clubs, (Lions, Rotary, and other events)? What do you do to make them Christian?

2. How do you, in your funeral ministry, balance the good news of eternal life in Christ with the fact of peoples' need to grieve?

Questions About You

1. When do you feel used by people the way that this pastor felt used? Sundays? Funerals? Weddings? Baptisms? Counseling? Home visits? Emergencies?
2. Why do you feel used? Have you ever told anyone this before now? When, or why not?
3. What's the difference between your letting off steam and being a cynic? Why might being a cynic hurt another Christian?
4. When do you find yourself being cynical?
5. With whom do you express your cynicism? How could this affect your ministry positively? Negatively?
6. Is there an evangelical role for the church in social or civic settings such as service clubs, scout troops, the military, birthday parties?
7. Why do you think people join a church?
8. Why are you a minister?

How Can Your Group Support You?

1. Can you recall historical or Biblical precedent for the type of ministry in your church about which you're feeling cynical? Does this help legitimize your ministry?
2. Does your group find the kingdom of God being served in their participation with civic or secular events? How so?
3. Define a strictly secular event. Define a strictly religious ministry. Can the two be combined?
4. Does your group have suggestions for seeing the good God works in everything for those who love him? Does this sound too pie-in-the-sky for you? Why?

5. How would you change your ministry or your perception of it? How can your group support you in your first step towards this change?

Meditation and Prayer Focus
Matthew 8:18-22

1. Jesus had a rough time and said so. Is this cynical?
2. How can you follow Jesus and also admit it's not easy without sounding cynical or whiney? Does this help you follow the Lord?
3. How will faith-active-in-love take your mind off ministerial worries and work for the kingdom to come to the end of the earth?

— 5 —
The Pool

Pitfall: You become discouraged in your evangelism efforts and tire of proclaiming the Gospel.

"We are fools for Christ's sake . . .
                                    1 Corinthians 4:10

The river flows over the cliffs to the jungle valley. The rushing white vertical water becomes silent green pools. The tall trees hold howler monkeys sleeping in the heat. The howlers have tired of watching the fisherman from the village. The monkeys sleep in the branches as green shadows possessing weight and breath.

The village men stand as still as the rocks which hold the pool. Hard toes cling to soft mossy rocks. Still spears are held above still faces. The men look below the surface of the water for the slow fish. Toes flex impatiently. This movement and blinking eyes are the only signs that the men are not oddly colored rocks on the edge of the still pool.

A hiss and a click break their communal trance. The warning signal comes from the old man. The men squat on the rocks, their spears pointed to the path.

The old man stands slowly. Sun filters through the leaves and turns to green the shadows on his face. His eyes relax their search of the jungle's depths. The old man spits. He says, "He's coming again."

The village men relax. They melt like red wax onto the rocks. They wait for the preacher to make his way along the trail. They stare into the water. The pool is still and green and deep. The water bugs and hot slow wind move its surface.

The pastor trips on a root. He falls hard on his side. He swears. A saw-like leaf has cut his hand. "A small cut like this can kill you in this putrid place," he mutters, his face down close to the mud.

He has taken to muttering often. At first he thought the mutterings to be prayer. But they are curses and confusions. The mutterings come from his tortured guts, burning feet and bleeding hands. At times his muttering clogs his throat and tires him as if he cannot take another breath. Now, in order to clear his throat he says clearly out loud, "It's not worth it!"

He stands patting away the mud and dirt from his clothes. A few angry twigs cling secretly in his hair.

The village men move to one side of the pool facing the pastor's approach. The pastor raises his hand. The villagers stand still. A fish jumps in the pool. The water noise is swallowed up in the green thirsty jungle.

The old man says, "Walk on the water, Christian."

The pastor stands facing the fishermen across the pool. Green birds and red birds and yellow birds fly silently above the men. The pool is like a plate of green bottle glass. "Just the color of a 7-Up bottle," thinks the pastor.

He speaks in the villagers' language, "You understand my words about my God, Don Jesus Cristo, as I understand your words about your life, your fishing. But you do not yet understand my God who fishes for you; that he might pull you up to his kingdom." The pastor heard the words he was speaking as if he were far away; far away in a cooler, cleaner place without the cloying closeness of the heat and his Lord.

"Walk on water, Christian. We pray to our rain god and he makes rain. We pray to our god of maize, we eat. Your god walks on water. You pray to your Don Jesus Cristo. Now you walk on water. Show us."

The pastor sees only curious expectation in the black eyes surrounding him. Golden sweat drips down the villagers' smooth foreheads. The veins move in their necks and arms. The warm jungle closeness, the pulses of the men, the barely rippling surface of the pool wait for him. And while waiting, these rhythms pass a daydream before the pastor's mind.

He remembers seminary where all was possible. The professors challenged his simple fragile faith. He had felt it stretched nearly to breaking. But the scholastic rigors had strengthened his faith, not made excuses for it. It had been a long time since he had believed in simple fragile miracles.

He steps onto the fragile surface of the pool. The green parts silently, and silently the Christian slips into the pool's warm depth. Under water he opens his eyes and sees green and black bubbles and his hands darting like pale fish which have forgotten how to swim.

He sinks into the maw of the jungle pool. The surrender to doubt enters his mind not as the expected stab of cold, but as a warm wave of relief, as warm as the pool water.

His feet touch bottom and he pushes off with his legs toward the surface following instinctively the rising bubbles. Breaking the surface, he is close to the edge of the pool. He finds a grip and pulls himself farther into the air. The villagers grab his arms and pull him out of the water as parents would lift their child from a bathtub.

The villagers' eyes shine with reflected sun from the jungle pool. The pastor oozes onto the mossy rocks. He catches his breath in gulps and lets it out in strange sharp cries. With his head down he smells and tastes the green depths of the water as it runs out his nose.

The old villager touches the pastor's shoulder. The pastor looks up at him and stands into the green sunlight.

The pastor says, "You see the faith Don Jesus Cristo gives me? I believe in him as the one true God. Miracles are not the only way God shows himself. So what if I sink with my faith? He gives me faith without giving me a miracle. That is a miracle in itself!"

A fish stirs the surface of the pool. The old man turns away from the Christian, then turns back again. "We admire you. But you have a foolish god." He turns back to the fish.

The pastor is not angry with these men who test him and his god. He wonders why he is not angry. It is not a matter of forgiveness exactly. Rather he seems too tired to be angry.

His head is full and tight. There is an empty looseness in his chest. Was it his words or his god which is unbelievable for them?

He rubs the water from his eyes. He looks at the villagers who look at him. His gaze passes through the still men to the jungle moving slightly in the wind. The green looks slippery and sharp and ready. This green will kill him by tiring him, by running him down as the villagers run down their prey in the chase.

The pastor focuses away from the green and back to the black of the villagers' eyes. They all turn away from him toward the pool. He turns and walks back through the jungle to the church's clearing in the jungle, the clearing scoured of the green.

The villagers look from the pool to one another. They are alone again. Their eyes are bright. The younger men laugh, their white teeth startle eyes accustomed to the jungle's green. The old man points to the pool with a jab of his spear. Quiet again, with birds flashing above them, the men enter their waiting trance.

The old man speaks as he stares down through the surface of the pool for the depths where the fish swim. "If the Christian comes back again with his god, then perhaps his god is not foolish; merely so the man. Yet if the fool does come back, maybe then we will begin to understand the power of this Christian's one true god."

Study and Reflection Guides For: The Pool

The Pastoral Pitfall: Being ridiculed for our faith in our resurrected and risen Lord; as "If for this life only we have hoped in Christ, we are of all [people] most to be pitied."

1 Corinthians 15:19

A Pastor's Insight: St. Paul:

"For I think that God has exhibited us apostles as last of all, . . . because we have become a spectacle to the world, to angels and [people]. We are fools for Christ's sake . . .".

1 Corinthians 4:9-10a

Questions About the Story

1. Why is the missionary pastor discouraged?
2. Why do the fishermen laugh at him?
3. Why does he feel the Lord's presence as cloying like the wet jungle heat?
4. Why does he step onto the water?
5. Why is doubt a relief for the pastor?
6. Does he really doubt his Lord?
7. How is sinking and rising in the pool like a baptism or like his seminary experience?
8. How will the villagers eventually be converted; by words or deeds or somehow else?

Questions About Your Ministry

1. How much of your day is spent talking about evangelism?
2. How much of your day is actually spent *doing* evangelism, i.e., talking about Christ's life, death, teachings, suffering, death, resurrection, ascension and presence?

3. How do you do evangelism? Door-to-door? From the pulpit? In the newspaper, television, radio? With church members only? How about with friends, relatives, strangers? At overtly churchy functions or socially too?
4. Do you have an evangelism committee? How effective are they? How faithful are they?
5. Do you have Invite-A-Friend Sundays at church?
6. How do your members see themselves as evangelists?
7. Is evangelism left up to you alone?

Questions About You

1. Do you ever get tired of, "Telling the old, old story of Jesus and his glory? When was the last time you told "the old, old story . . ."?
2. When was the last time you were tired of telling it? Why?
3. When do you feel foolish talking God-talk? How could you be more natural and authentic in your witness?
4. Have you ever been a street-preacher, a chaplain in the Armed Services, or given an invocational prayer at a secular meeting? How did you feel? Did you use different words then those you normally use in church on Sunday? Why?
5. Do you get nervous before preaching?

How Can Your Group Support You?

1. Does your group have special evangelism methods that are effective?
2. Are there books that can be recommended to motivate the shy or discouraged evangelist?
3. Consider role-playing as evangelists in difficult or silly situations. Have fun and discuss what seemed to work and not work? What seemed real and authentic to the persons involved? What seemed fake, overly pious, wooden or rehearsed?

Meditation and Prayer Focus
Matthew 25:21
(Or the entire parable of the wise and foolish servants.)

1. We are called to be servants of the Lord. How can we best serve him according to this parable?
2. How can evangelism be seen as caring for our Lord's talents?
3. We are to be faithful servants and effective as well. How can our faithfulness be effective?
4. What is the danger of looking for effectiveness in our faithful service to the Lord? Too much concern for our personal works righteousness? Too much concern with numbers and not relationships in the parish?
5. How can Jesus help us to see our evangelical call as being one of relationships in his name and not a numbers game?
6. How does Jesus relate to you as your master? Does this personal relationship give you any idea about how to love other people through your authority as a called and ordained minister?
7. With your group, talk over your personal feelings about your relationship with your Lord and Master, Jesus. Try to not use any faith-formulas, God-talk, jargon or trite phrases. Focus on now.
8. Make these feelings, hopes and fears part of your closing prayers.

— 6 —
A Trick

Pitfall: You use empty faith phrases
in difficult situations, thus failing
to minister to peoples' needs.

"I have become all things to all [people], that I might by all means save some."
1 Corinthians 9:22

It is a pleasant enough prison. The powers-that-be painted the walls pink because it is supposed to make us inmates less aggressive and less depressed.

So, I'm not depressed. But the pink walls don't help my fear of death. I'll be killed soon. I'm scared. I don't want to look like a scared jerk in front of the official witnesses and my family.

I just want to get it over with; like a race around the high school track. Winning was never that important. I never won. But I always wanted to run; to run and get it over with.

I always let life kind of just happen to me. And soon, death is going to happen to me; a state execution by due process of law.

The chaplain is coming. The sheriff is with him to let him in to the cell. I see only a few people each day. Each person has his own talisman of identity. The sheriff announces himself with the echo of jingling keys in the concrete hallway. The chaplain will smell like books or candles no doubt. I notice that as death approaches my own identity is shrinking. I am even starting to hunch over — trying to make myself smaller so death can't find me trapped in this cell. My talisman is my sweat of fear.

The chaplain is let in. He sits down and just sits there. He feels silly being here. I'm a killer who has never come to his chapel services or asked him to come to my cell. He once delivered a Bible and asked to talk to me, but I tossed the tiny black book back to him.

The chaplain is wearing street clothes that seem out-of-date. He's worn these civilian clothes to relate to me, no doubt. The pewter cross around his neck gives him away as a chump. He looks silly and uncomfortable, like a relative come to visit an ailing relation with nothing really to say and only a distant love somewhere in the past making a connection between them.

The chaplain sits on the bunk leaning away from me with his back against the cool pink wall. I'm sitting on a short stool bolted to the floor. He says, "No chance of a pardon from the governor. Looks like the end."

I feel my jaw get tight. I want to punch him. I say, "No doubt. You're right. Death is thirty feet from me, but only about four feet from you. So watch yourself, I haven't got anything to lose now."

The chaplain's chin has razor burn the same pink as the walls. His chin quivers a bit. He says, "You have more to lose than I do. Save your eternal spirit. See the love of God for you even now. Turn to Jesus who is here for you. He will give you the gift of faith you need to turn to him. Be saved from your sin and death." He leans back as if relieved of this message's burden.

He's memorized this desperate little last-minute plea. I too have memorized my speech before death, "Let's get it over with," I'll say.

I say to the chaplain, "Okay. I'll believe. But first I want to see Jesus bend these bars and let me out of here. Then I'll believe in God. Or a telephone call from the governor, telling me I'm forgiven and inviting me over to his mansion for dinner."

"Whether you die today or twenty years from today, you still need to see Jesus with you. You are a child of God in his eyes. The miracle is that God loves you right now. See how God is turning your heart to him." The chaplain's eyes don't meet mine.

The chaplain is leaning forward from the bunk. His cross is dangling around his neck like the rope that will be dangling around mine. I could reach out and pull his chain tight across his neck. Instead, I lean away from him against my wall. I ask, "Don't you ever get tired of pretending that there is a God?"

"Yes, I do get tired of pretending there is a God." The chaplain's eyes are looking at mine.

I sit straight up on my stool. I stand up. My finger points at his cross. My words come out fast as I shout, "You dare come here with a cross around your scrawny neck to comfort a man who is sentenced to die and instead you tell me you only pretend to believe in the God you say loves me?"

The chaplain recoils back to his wall. "I said, that I was tired of pretending there is a God. Sometimes I feel that I just go through the motions of faith without being totally convinced it makes a difference. Whether I pretend, though, God is real and you and I have to deal with him."

My legs are oddly weak. I feel the power of anger in my shoulders, but my knees are wobbly as though I'd just run a race, as though I'd just run from something frightening. I sit back down on the stool. "So, you're not sure about this God either?" The chaplain has grabbed my fear and held it for me to see.

"Yes. I'm not sure. I mean, why doesn't he bend those bars when you ask him? Why doesn't the governor suddenly have it come into his mind that you're a swell guy and pardon you and invite you over to meet his daughter and have dinner?"

I look at the bars, the play of light on the cell floor from the light bulb in the hall. The stripes of shadow and light fall across my shoes and trousers and I imagine across my face as well. "I guess I'm proof of God not really being able to do anything to help his children. I lived a crummy life. I'm going to die a crummy death."

The chaplain sighs from his nose, a hummed moan of agreement. "Hm, you took advantage of your free will to reject God. He gave you that freedom to not love him, because he loves you so."

"Loves me? You said you don't know if God is real." The chaplain is starting to really get on my nerves. What good is a chaplain without answers? "How do you know about God's love for me?"

"Jesus is God. He tells us he is with us always, until the end of the age. I trust him and his promise. I don't exactly know it as much as I trust it — the whole thing." The cross is twisting on its chain. Its spidery shadow falls among the webs of the bars' shadows that lay over me.

I say to him, "So you live your goody-goody life thinking that there might be a God. And I live my life like God isn't around to notice." I lean towards him and jab my finger at him. "You pretend to be good and make a living off people. I deceive them until I can con them. There is not much of a difference between us. We both make money off peoples' trusting our pretenses. I'm just more down-to-earth than you."

The chaplain rubs his hands on his pants. "In a way, you're right. I may tell people God is their all-powerful, loving Father, but all they have to do is open their eyes to the evil and disease in the world to call me a liar."

"So, I call you a liar. You're a liar. No doubt about it."

The chaplain smiles. "You've made some progress. At least you're not calling God a liar by blaming him for your predicament."

"You're really bugging me, man." The power has come back to my legs. My forehead feels hard and hot and my breath is short and fast. I really could hurt this guy. "Why are you here with me? Is your coming here to the cell of a dead man some kind of perverted good-luck charm for you? Some good deed for extra credit? Are you just hedging your bets in case there is this big bearded dude up in the clouds? Just playing it safe in case Jesus really does love you in spite of your doubt?"

"Yes, in a way. I came here as a discipline. I know how foolish this might seem to you. Even St. Paul noted that we Christians are fools if this Jesus thing turns out to be a fairy tale. Yet, St. Paul was given the grace to keep the faith. I hope to keep mine."

"Yeah," I say. "It always seemed to me that you Christians were playing it safe. If Jesus is there and you believe in him and have a good life, you win heaven. If Jesus is there and you have a crummy life, you still win heaven. If Jesus isn't there and you believe in him and have a good or crummy life and end up dead as a mackerel, you still win because you go out looking good to the end."

"Why don't you?" the chaplain says.

"Why don't I what?"

"Why don't you go out looking good to the end?"

"You mean," I ask, "why don't I take a chance that there is a God? It seems a last-minute kind of deal. Will it count? I can't exactly be a Boy Scout between now and, . . . you know."

The chaplain leans towards me. We're both leaning forward now. I feel he's a little too close, but I want to hear his words. "Yes, your faith will still count, even now in this place. Christ is here. He'll accept your doubt with your faith. He accepted the last-minute trust of a thief who died next to him. Believe in this illusive, loving God. That's the trick."

"Some trick," I say and lean back. "Some trick. God has me jump through his hoop of faith and land in his eternal kingdom where I live surrounded by his love forever, even after death. All because of Jesus. It's that easy, no doubt."

"Something like that, yes. As a matter of fact, that's it exactly," the chaplain says and leans back against the wall.

"But even you don't always, constantly believe in him!"

"As I said," the chaplain replies, "that's the trick."

Study and Reflection Guides For:
A Trick

The Pastoral Pitfall: Using empty faith phrases in difficult situations, thus failing to minister to peoples' needs through listening and serving them in their need.

A Pastor's Insight: "If I speak in the tongues of people and of angels, but have not love, I am a noisy gong or a clanging cymbal."

1 Corinthians 13:1

Questins About the Story

1. Why do you think the chaplain says a speech to the convict? Why might you be tempted to do the same? Is this being like a clanging cymbal?
2. Is the chaplain a chump in visiting and trying to convert the prisoner?
3. What is the distant love that may connect the chaplain and prisoner as visiting relatives?
4. Does the chaplain succeed in reaching the prisoner with the gospel? Why or why not? How does the chaplain finally show the prisoner that he is listening to his fear and doubt? Is this a part of Christian love?
5. The prisoner keeps saying, "No doubt." How does the chaplain use the prisoner's doubt to bring him closer to faith? Would Paul have enslaved himself to this doubt in order to win the prisoner? (cf: 1 Corinthians 9:19)
6. In the prisoner's words, "What good is a chaplain without answers"? Was the chaplain any good for the prisoner?

Questions About Your Ministry

1. Do you use formulas in your evangelical ministry?
2. Does your church tradition or confessional teaching or dogma use formulas of faith? What are some you've memorized? Why did you memorize them?
3. Do you adapt your teaching and preaching to your audience? How?
4. How do you let go of people who do not or will not listen to your evangelical message or who lapse or backslide? Should you let go of them?

Questions About You

1. Do you, like the chaplain, ever feel you are pretending there is a God? How are you ministered to in regard to keeping alive and active your service to God?
2. Have you ever been personally responsible for winning a soul?
3. The chaplain wears a cross. What do you do to let the public know you are a minister of the gospel?
4. To whom do you express your faith-struggles and doubts?
5. How do you define a minister? When do you know you are ministering to someone? When do you really feel you are a minister? What do you like best about ministry? Least?

How Can Your Group Support You?

1. Share some awkward or challenging evangelical moments you have experienced.
   a. With the poor.
   b. With the sick and or dying.
   c. With cynics/skeptics.
   d. With people who have ministered to you.
2. What would you do differently now?
3. Tell how you have been like someone in order to save them. Did you feel like a fake or like an empathetic minister?

Meditation and Prayer Focus
1 Peter 2:1-3

1. When have you tasted the kindness of the Lord?
2. How does this kindness taste? How were you nourished with this pure spiritual milk?
3. How would you share this nourishment with others?
4. How can faith-formulas, dogmas and evangelical gimmickry be guileful and insincere?
5. What is the essence of ministering with this kindness of the Lord: love, hope, patience, sincerity, honesty, endurance, effectiveness?
6. Do you consider yourself one of the newborn babes or a grown-up in regard to salvation? Why? How mature is your kindness? How child-like is your faith?
7. What would you like to be when you are grown up to salvation? Make these hopes part of your closing prayer.

— 7 —
In The Trenches

Pitfall: Your ministry becomes mechanical.
You see yourself as a cog in the machine.
People come to you
as a dispenser of good luck.

> . . . but they had certain points of dispute with him about their superstition and about one Jesus, . . .
> Acts 25:19a

The canary had awakened Mac. It was good to hear. It meant another morning and no mustard gas in the trenches of Verdun. Mac was expecially afraid of gas attacks because he lost his gas mask in the previous day's fighting. He hadn't been issued a new one yet. Supply lines weren't so great in this Great War.

Mac turned towards the songbird. With no proper diet the canary had lost much of its color. Everything turned to grey in the mud of the churned-up battlefield. No trees, no life — just barbed wire, fog and muddy faces. Some of the faces were alive. Some of the faces would appear through the mud when it rained or when you dug a hole to hide in.

The bird sang with a fluidity that was in contrast with the mechanical chatter of a heavy machine-gun in the enemy trenches a quarter-mile away. So many new machines to kill with; the tank, the flying machine, the machine-gun, gas attacks. The songbird could warn of a mechanically produced death, but the machines could kill the song, poison the air through which the song once flew and even clatter their way into flight.

Louis was at Mac's side, awake since the machine-gun opened up. Louis was watching the chaplain feed the canary. "The padre takes good care of him," he observed.

The chaplain had become "padre" even though he wasn't a Roman father, but a Lutheran pastor. The men assumed he was Catholic and after awhile the pastor had given up explaining. Just as there were no atheists in foxholes, so denominational lines tended to blur and lose their importance when death came so near, so often.

To the pastor, the men too had begun to blur from their individual sufferings. He thought of them as one raw wound. He thought, "How can Christ keep track of all this suffering? Wasn't his own enough misery for God? Maybe this suffering was too much for God and now He refuses to feel our pain anymore?"

He fed the bird. It seemed to sing even as it breathed — a musical toot with each breath of its life. It hopped back and forth in its cage. The pastor did not let it become a pet. It was merely a delicate indicator of deadly gas in the air. If the gas attack came, the canary would die first and warn the soldiers to put on their masks. The pastor fed the delicate feathered machine. He fed it without thinking just as he fed the men the mechanism of the liturgy; . . . "The body and blood of our Lord, Amen."

The pastor put the birdcage in the forward trench nearest the enemy. It was a day without a predictable wind and therefore there was little chance of a gas attack. The ground fog was the only reason to suspect a silent march of grey ghosts crawling towards this side of No Man's Land. The bird hopped in the brass cage, strumming the thin bars that emitted a sound like an out-of-tune harp.

The bird sang as the pastor waded back to his cave in the trench wall. He wedged past the men who had become a type of delicate mud-machine. The men's faces had become blank and machine-like by the pure boredom of the trenches; by the fear and waiting that weighed them down and stuck to them like the mud that piled up on the bottom of their boots.

The padre had become a machine too. As a result, religious services, when attended at all, were attended for the mechanics of good luck. It was hard enough to preach God's love when God seemed absent from the long suffering and sudden death in the mud. But also, a circumstance beyond the padre's control had changed the padre from a mere representative of God's love in the world into something of more positive worth in the eyes of the troops. He was now a talisman of dumb luck.

The padre had become a good-luck charm by nearly being killed. Two months ago he had been sent "over the top" with the troops. He was to accompany the corpsman as a stretcher-bearer. The corpsman was saddled with medical supplies, the padre with communion wine, hosts, olive oil, a Bible, their food and rifles. The sergeant's whistle blew and over the top of the trench they stood. The corpsman went first, lifting the stretcher over the wire. The padre came behind, muttering prayers and pulling at his boot to free it from the deep mud.

As the padre pulled his boot free and stood up, a bullet hit the padre square in the helmet and knocked him back into the trench. The corpsman fell forward with the stretcher on the other side of the wire and made it to a foxhole.

After the assault, the men found the padre alive and dazed. The bullet had entered his helmet, neatly pierced his scalp, roared around the outside of his skull and exited inside his helmet to drop under his collar as a grey lump of lead, like a piece of mud that had been tossed down his shirt by a prankster.

The troops thought his luck miraculous. Their acclaim focused more on their hope of a generally dispensible good fortune than on the padre's individually appropriated miracle.

Now, this foggy morning, as the pastor sat down alone, he saw the ducking and turning of heads down the long line of the trench as a message was passed man to man. An assault would begin soon. The officers probably expected an enemy assault in this fog and might as well stage one of their own. With the assault planned, the ritual would soon begin for good luck. The pastor wanted to stand up and have something to say to the men who would come to him, but he knew he would just sit and let them do their ritual.

The ritual had begun with the mens' manly slaps on the padre's back. Touching him was like touching a good luck charm. Soon the ritual was formalized and included a dozen or more men shyly and quietly lining up to file past him and lay a hand on his shoulder or scarred forehead. The pastor had tried to tell the men of their error, but the phenomenon had its own logic and power. They listened to his well-reasoned warnings and then silently lined up to touch him the next time an assault was readied to go over the top.

The pastor saw the men checking their equipment for the assault, shifting around in nervousness and getting into an informal line to touch him. The touches were no longer flippant pats but reverent caresses. The pastor's eyes watched the mud as the men filed past and touched his shoulder or head. He felt that with each touch the men were pushing him closer to the mud.

A scouting patrol was sent out before the main assault. Mac and Louis were separated during the main assault later that day. The men were driven back to the trench without having gained an inch of No Man's Land. Upon their return, they fell asleep at once.

They slept fitfully, dreaming of flashing bayonets and rusted barbed wire, mountains of exploding mud. Each called out the other's name in their sleep.

The next morning Mac was awakened by the canary. The sky was clear. Louis was awake beside him eating something. Far away, a flying machine buzzed as if taunting the caged bird.

Louis asked, "Did you hear about the padre?"

Mac had heard, but Louis was usually more accurate with the stories than others. Mac replied, "No. Tell me."

"Well, remember they sent out a scouting patrol before our main assault yesterday? The men in the patrol had come by to touch the padre the way they do. The big skinny guy,

Dannels, he touched him three times; for himself, his wife and his kid . . ."

". . . Anyway, off they go over the top, slinking away into the fog. Along about noon the fog was still thick and the patrol hadn't returned. We figure they had been captured. The padre was pacing up and down like he could do something for them, like it was his fault. He kept rubbing his hands like he was cold, like the mud was seeping into his skin. He even had turned kind of grey like the mud and his eyes were just dirty puddles. He kept rubbing his hands and arms and shoulders and pacing in the trenches."

Louis looked at Mac and up into the sky. The aeroplane was circling, an artillery spotter maybe. If it were an enemy plane, shells would start falling soon.

Louis continued, "Around one o'clock the fog was still with us. The assault might be called off. We couldn't just go charging blindly in the fog, groping around until we fell into the enemy trench. Then, out of the fog comes a voice. It's Dannels. He's crying for his mom and everything. It's like barbed wire cutting you to hear him crying out in the mud somewhere. The fog is confusing our ears and we can't really tell where he might be, or how far out there. And he sobs and all."

Mac can see Louis is back in the morning, back with the phantom cries in the fog.

"Meanwhile the padre is just about to have a fit. He's all by himself and we all are letting him be. I thought of talking to him, but he was so agitated, rubbing himself and all. I could hear him mutter, 'Let me alone,' like he was busy praying or something. So I left him alone." Louis takes a bite of food and gulps some coffee. His breath steams when he talks.

"The fog finally cleared. The sobbing had stopped and all was quiet. The sun punched through the clouds and that canary started to chirp, real sharp like, and that sent the padre over the top of the trench toward where he thought Dannels' crys had come." Louis lifted his eyes from the mud to Mac. "The enemy had set us up. Some guy on the other side knew English real good. The bullet caught the padre almost exactly in the same spot the first one had. He was back dead in the trench a second after he left it. He tried to bring the patrol some extra luck and ran out of it when he needed it most."

Mac sighed. The plane had left the sky. Fog was rising again from the soaked ground. The fog would delay the artillery bombardments for another day. He had more time to dig deeper into the mud before death fell from the sky.

Louis said, "You know what's kind of odd . . . what the guys found in the padre's stuff? He was wearing his dog tags and a cross, of course. He had his old pocket Bible. And he had a rabbit's foot, with all the fur rubbed off. You ever see a rabbit's foot without the fur? It's an ugly little thing."

Study and Reflection Guides For:
In The Trenches

The Pastoral Pitfall: Your worship becomes mechanical. People come to you and your worship service for good luck.

A Pastor's Insight: "Human nature is idolatrous and superstitious; it flees from the true God, and promotes confidence in its own brand of worship and its own works."
Martin Luther

Questions About the Story

1. What does the canary represent in the story?
2. What does the mud symbolize for you in the story?
3. What made the soldiers and pastor mechanical?
4. What made the pastor's religious services mechanical?
5. The men used the pastor as a rabbit's foot. Why?
6. How do you think the pastor saw himself and his situation as he went over the top for the last time?
7. Did the story remind you of any superstitions you or your parishioners practice?

Questions About Your Ministry

1. Why do people come to your church services?
2. What special thing does your church service have to offer people that they cannot find elsewhere?
3. How do you keep your worship service fresh and alive?
4. What is the advantage of having a set liturgy?
5. What is the disadvantage?
6. What do you find most important in your liturgy?
7. What do the people find most important?
8. About what aspects of worship do you get the most complaints?

9. How can you help solve the complaints? Should they be solved or should you keep tradition as is? Why?
10. What could you take or leave in your liturgy?

Questions About You

1. How do you deal with the stress of ministering with the Good News in the midst of day-to-day bad news?
2. How is your faith like hoping for good luck?
3. How is it different?
4. How do you see yourself as a minister? A priest? A symbol of God's love present in the world? A servant? A good-luck charm? Moral virtuoso? Business person?
5. How many ways have you been seen by people who came to you as a representative of Christ's church? Did you clarify their preconceptions of your role, identity, or function as a minister of the gospel and sacraments?
6. Do you have experience in ministry under violent situations? Share with the others the difference of ministry in violent situations versus ministry in peaceful situations.

How Can Your Group Support You?

1. Visit one another's worship services. Critique what felt alive and what felt wooden during the service. Critique how the people seemed, as well as the mechanics of the service. Watch for how people acted before, during and after the service.
2. Share sermon/service critiques that your worship committee, pulpit committee or pastoral support committee may use to give you feedback.
3. Share your perceptions of how you see your colleagues.
    a. Address their gifts.
    b. Address their hurts.

Meditation and Prayer Focus
James 5:11-12

1. How have you seen the purpose of the Lord in your life recently?
2. When was the last time you questioned the purpose of the Lord? Did you handle your dilemma mechanically?
3. Are there hard times now that make it hard for you to be steadfast in the faith? When was the last time you were not steadfast?
4. Did the Lord's compassion and mercy help you to remain steadfast or did you just muscle through on your own?
5. How can relying on yourself be a sort of superstition?
6. When have you failed to say, "Yes," or "No," plainly?
7. How did this failure put you under condemnation?
8. How did you get free of this condemnation?
9. How will you avoid relying on yourself or dumb-luck and instead rely on our Lord the next time you're so tempted?

— 8 —
Beloved

Pitfall: Your Christian love and compassion is misunderstood as sexual seduction.

Beloved, let us love one another; for love is of God, and he who loves is born of God and knows God.
1 John 4:7

When one counsels people who are despairing of God's love, it is a good idea to keep one's chair away from the door. One doesn't want to be trampled when they flee from God or their sin or the embarrassment of their confession.

I had moved my chair away from the door as the young woman confessed to me her dilemma: "I want to be loved by you," she said. She stared at me and crossed her legs. My chair squeaked as I sat bolt upright. I think I let out a squeak too. I wished my chair were closer to the door.

She was one of those people who seem always to be searching. They have the wrinkled brow, the keen eyes, the forward-leaning posture of a seeker-of-something. They are the opposite of content. They are nomadic, foragers, gleaners. When they move they move to take something and put it somewhere else, or to consume it and move on.

I said, "You have my love as a brother in Christ. As St. John said, 'Beloved, let us love one another.' "

She said, "Baloney. I want you to love me as a man. When you baptized me last month, didn't you feel me move my head up under your hand?" She leaned in her chair and winked or blinked or did something with her face. I missed it exactly, and was glad I did.

I said, "I think you're confused about the love we have to share. It is God's love. I didn't so much baptize you as God truly did. You were baptized. God is your God and you are God's beloved child. He bestowed his Word, his Spirit, his love on you. I just recalled these promises, helping you to see God's love for you."

I was taking a coward's refuge in sacramental theology. I was back-pedaling and throwing words at her. The bigger and more complicated the words and thoughts, the better.

She snipped cleanly through my Biblical barbed-wire, "But I love you. You're the only person who treats me the way you do. You listen to me, you take time for me, you are honest with me, you reflect my opinions to me and let me see myself, you take the chance of being vulnerable with me." She was leaning forward. My chair squeaked again. I remembered that the window was behind me and coyly scooted my chair over to it like a scuttling crab sinking in wet sand.

I said, "This vulnerable, patient, forgiving and giving love you sense is the love of our Lord."

I didn't have much conviction this truth was going to work. She didn't want to hear about God's love, which gives itself to others. She wanted to hear about love that takes, about love that shares itself only so it can have as much as it gives, and maybe more.

Continuing, I spoke rapidly, "God comes to us as true man. He was tempted but never sinned, so that his sinlessness would be bestowed on us when he sacrificed himself through God's self-giving love. Our Lord is the humble one, not me. He is the understanding one, not me. He's the one who helps us confess our sin and see ourselves as we really are. He leads us to repentence and forgiveness and our inheritance as his beloved children."

She wasn't buying it. "You keep holding a mask of Jesus in front of your human love. Why don't you just plain ol' love me?"

I was out of breath. I took a breath. "When you see the love of a Christian and feel that love, you are seeing and feeling the love of the Lord. Martin Luther said we should all strive to be little Christs."

"So, I'm in love with Jesus, not you? Don't you think you're a bit of a braggart? That's like saying that because you try to be like Paul Newman, I've fallen in love with you because you're now Paul Newman and not yourself and I can't tell the difference." She leaned back, pleased with her logic.

I told her, "In the New Testament, one of the signs of the church was how the new Christians loved one another. This didn't mean they were all dating one another in some first century Christian-Singles' Club. The way the Christians loved one another was the way other folks knew the Christians were Christians and not some free-love cult. They loved one another with God's love. The love that gives of itself freely, no strings attached but to share the love received for Christ's sake.

She affected a pout. It surprised me to see her face without the hard look I had always seen before. But I was suspicious of the pout anyway. She charmingly mumbled through it, "But I thought God's love *was* free love."

I felt as though I were in a hall-of-mirrors. I felt as though I kept holding up a sign clearly labeled with the word LOVE and the comic-mirrors kept reflecting, SEX. Nearly pouting myself, I said, "God's love is free and freeing to give of itself. God gave himself, his only begotten Son to die for us. He gives himself in love and forgiveness in the waters of baptism and in the bread and wine of his body and blood. John writes of Jesus' own words, "A new commandment I give you, that you love one another; even as I have loved you, that you love one another." So, we're freed from our selfish sin to selflessly love one another. Not take love, not even share love, but to give love to one another, more than we receive."

"Pooh," she pouted. "You *don't* love me. You'll never love me." She started to cry. "This has been such a terrible misunderstanding! I thought you really loved me. You were to kind, so available, so approachable, so attentive, so forgiving. You were just being Christ-like. Why couldn't you just be a real man?" She cried as she ran out the door.

Study and Reflection Guides For: Beloved

Pastoral Pitfall: Having your Christ-like concern and love misunderstood as being sexual in nature.

A Pastor's Insight: "Our faith and sacrament must not rest on a person — be he good or bad, ordained or unordained, called or self-appointed (*eigneschlichen*), the devil or his mother — but on Christ, on His Word, on His office, on His command and ordinance. Wherever these are observed, matters must be and go right, no matter who or what the person who administers them may be."

Martin Luther

Questions About the Story

1. The counselor is surprised. Could he have seen this coming before this meeting?
2. How could he have prevented this misunderstanding? Was it an unavoidable circumstance?
3. Did he avoid the problem or minister to his parishioner?
4. What do you think will happen the next time they meet?
5. What if the pastor had been female and the parishioner male? How might things have been the same or different?

Questions About Your Ministry

1. Have you ever had your Christian love mistaken for sexual love? How did you handle the misunderstanding?
2. How do you handle the aspect of confidentiality if the parishioner were to gossip? Would you tell your side of the misunderstanding to the parish, to the church council, to your clergy support group or confessor?

3. How much counseling do you do? What academic degrees do you have that somehow legitimize the counseling you do?
4. Does your church carry malpractice insurance?
5. In what ways do people project their feelings about the church, Jesus, and God onto the person of the pastor?

Questions About You

1. How do you deal with parishioners who project their personal problems and hopes onto you as a savior, a saint, a persecutor, servant or judge?
2. How would you like to be seen as a person?
3. How do you think the parishioners see you?
4. Are you alone when you counsel others in the church?
5. What about house calls?
6. What precautions do you take in your counseling?
   a. To maintain privacy and confidentiality?
   b. To keep the counseling space open and approachable to the public when counseling so as to avoid the suspicion of intimate meetings of a sexually charged nature?
7. Is the above question old-fashioned or silly? Why or why not?

How Can Your Group Support You?

1. Do they have recommendations for continuing education courses dealing with professional counseling techniques?
2. Do they have books on pastoral care to recommend?
3. Do you know professionals with whom you can work and to whom you may refer parishioners?
4. Share together your typical counseling setting and session. How often and for how many sessions do you typically meet?
5. Visit one another's offices and counseling areas. Suggest ways to keep the space open and yet private.

Meditation and Prayer Focus
Romans 8:5-17

1. Is this chapter too ascetic for you? Why or why not?
2. "... to set the mind on the Spirit is life and peace." (v. 7b) How can this verse guide you in your counseling?
3. How can life and peace be means of revealing to people their projections or misunderstandings about you, their family members, spouses, other therapists or Christ and his church?
4. How can the Spirit of God in you, give you peace and life?
5. How does your group support one another in peace and life?
6. Ask in your prayers for specific needs in your life to be filled with the peace and life of the Spirit.
7. Ask your group members how you can support them with peace and life right now, later in the week, at your next meeting.

— 9 —
The Sacrifice

Pitfall: People see worship at church as a good work that will earn them the reward of heaven.

. . . He said, "It is finished"; and he bowed his head and gave up his spirit.

John 19:30

Light and dust blew in through the window of my library study. The light was hot and the dust plugged up my nose, made me breath through my mouth and covered my teeth with grit. The dust was in my eyes and scratched them as I scanned the text. The light made the page too brilliant to read. I kissed the book and put the Greek New Testament down on my desk.

"It is finished," I thought, was better translated as, "It is fulfilled." "Finished," was so permanent. It was as if Jesus' mission on earth were done and that was that; a few years of teaching and then the lethal betrayal of a disgruntled student.

The word, "fulfilled," on the lips of the dying Christ, gave a hint that all creation was not doomed by his murder. We could still hope for a way out of our own death, even after killing God's Son.

It was too bright and hot to concentrate. Early morning was the only time the wind didn't blow down the village street. With the sun rising over the plains, the dry wind got moving and sought the cool river and the mountain shadows far away. I left the hot bright study and retreated to the cool dark sanctuary to prepare for the morning prayer service.

I entered the tiny sacristy; the closet-sized room that I use to change into my robes and in which I say my prayers in secret to my God who is in secret. The acolyte was dressed in his red cassock and white cotta. The whiteness was yellowed by years of dry wind and perspiration. He helped me with my cassock and surplice. He went out to make sure that the altar was dressed in the right color for the church season.

"Purple," he said. The sharp smell of incense clung to his robes. I put on my purple stole and we went out to worship with the early risers and pray with them the sad prayers of Lent.

Lenten prayers are short and bittersweet, almost mocking in their pious sing-songs for help and assurance from this God who let his only Son die for us. "Look at us," we cry, "You didn't help your Son until it was too late for his mortal life! Help us now in ours!"

The service ended quickly and the villagers drifted away in the low winter sun. I walked the length of the church to the big front doors and watched the villagers leave.

They walked up the hill alone or with one partner. Through the brilliant white dust that puffed about them like clouds, they floated upwards, as if I had entertained some of Paul's angels unawares. These angels left long shadows lingering in the sanctuary as they walked from the church and into the sun.

I had never noticed angels to cast shadows in the classic paintings that I had studied. The paintings of the annunciation or such. I counted the shadows and villagers to make sure they added up. I was disappointed when the shadows and figures added up the same.

One villager-angel lingered in the shadow of the sanctuary. Lucius limped over to me. His crooked shape was like a fallen angel who had crumpled to earth. He clung to my robes in order to balance himself and leaned from the shadows into the light. He was young and strong, and mutilated by his desire to be holy. He allowed himself to be nailed to a cross each year on Good Friday.

He mumbled his request, "Pastor, I have come for your prayers." His head was cast down as if he were holding in his tightly clamped hands a faith that had to be watched lest it dart away.

I was no longer shocked at his gory annual duty. I was no longer shocked at our human lust for our own spilled blood. But I was still surprised at his annual asking of my prayerful permission.

"No, Lucius, I will not pray for you. I have told you again and again not to sacrifice yourself." He clung more heavily on my robes. I continued, "I have told the villagers, the mayor too. I have told the doctor. I have gone to your mother. I have written my bishop."

We weren't looking at one another. Our thoughts were hostile and we were unsure of how to speak passionately in the doorway of the church. Lucius leaned on me more heavily. His head was against my side and his whining voice came from the folds of my robes. He spoke as if to himself, in a voice with no authority.

"But it is expected of me. The people and I have agreed. It is important."

A fly buzzed into the cool sanctuary and landed on my sleeve. It cleaned its feet and hands on me. "God does not need your sacrifice," I said. "Once was enough. Jesus died once and for all, for one and all. God does not need you up on the cross each year."

Again, that mumbled humility that now was as proud as a bully's boasting, "But the people need me up on the cross. The people need the sacrifice. The people need me."

"Don't fool yourself," I said looking at him. "You need them. You need to be up on the cross each year. What good is Jesus if you insist on taking his place? You lead people astray. They see you, Lucius on that cross, not the Son of God on the cross at Golgotha."

The little man limped over to lean on the doorway. He slipped down and sat on the cool concrete. As he turned his profile to the light I could see the scars dug in his forehead from the crown of thorns he annually wore. He looked up at me. He said, "You sacrifice Jesus again and again on Sunday.

Every Sunday he comes down from heaven and seeps into the bread and you tear him into pieces. He is patient with your abuse." His forehead and jaws were taut with rage, his eyes wrinkled with sadness and questions.

I answered with a careful cadence, "You might like to look into the chalice some day. Your gaze won't float in blood, but in wine. You can come into the sacristy after communion and sift the bread crumbs for bones if you like." I was looking away, out into the brilliant street. "I don't *re*-sacrifice flesh and blood. I *re*-call Jesus' promise that the bread is his body and the wine his blood and that he died once for our sins. He is there *for* us, but not for us to sacrifice with bloody, sticky hands. He is there, present to us in order to help us now that he is risen from his one death. He isn't like some magic jack-in-the-box you can put back into the tomb and enjoy his popping out again and again."

"Maybe for you. Maybe for God. But not for us," Lucius was shouting in the echoing sanctuary. "You tell us that Jesus is God. Yet he suffered only three hours. My wife has suffered in her lungs and bones for six years. God didn't suffer enough for his groaning creation! Why do you think the people keep coming here to worship, to see Jesus sacrificed over and over again because once was enough? Ha. They come for revenge!"

Lucius raised himself as he said this. He limped away quickly, crookedly into the square, too proud to have crutches or even a cane. My prayers went after him, trying to keep up through the bitter dust he was raising with his shuffle.

I watched him move across the village square. Lucius cast no shadow as the dust he raised clouded his threatening retreat toward his cross.

Study and Reflection Guides For: The Sacrifice

The Pastoral Pitfall: You are attacked personally by people who see your pastoral care of "salvation by grace through faith," as an obstacle on their private road to salvation.

A Pastor's Insight: ". . . we can't be persuaded [by our reason] that God gives his Son and loves us so much . . . That God is so merciful, not on account of my works but on account of his Son, is incomprehensible."
Martin Luther as recorded by Veit Dietrich, November 30, 1532

Questions About the Story

1. What translation of Christ's last words ("it is finished," or "it is fulfilled,") is most reflective of Lucius' despair and anger? What about the pastor's point of view.?
2. Why does Lucius think Jesus didn't suffer enough?
3. Why does Lucius go up on his cross each year?

Questions About Your Ministry

1. Why do you think people come to your services week after week or ask for your ministering to them week after week?
2. How do your Lenten ministries help people see Jesus' great sacrifice for them?
3. How might these services lead people to think that they are the ones making sacrifices to God? To the church? To you?
4. When did you last see or hear someone credit their works as meriting salvation?
5. How did you address this confusion?

Questions About You

1. In your opinion and/or experience, how does salvation work?
    a. Are you passively given salvation through a bestowed grace of God?
    b. Are you given a grace that helps you participate in your salvation with good works?
    c. Are you predestined by God for salvation or damnation?
    d. What do you teach and preach? What do you really think? If there is a difference, address the reasons for this and ask the group their opinion.
2. How have you ignored God's grace and tried to work your way to heaven?

How Can Your Group Support You?

1. Name some typical works of righteousness that you've seen.
2. How have you acted in the same way?
3. Can anyone in the group help you to avoid these acts?
4. What might be the beneficial results of these acts?
5. Make a top ten list of these works and talk about how to dedicate their energy in thankfulness to God.

Meditation and Prayer Focus
Romans 5:1-4

1. How do you experience the peace with God through your Lord Jesus Christ?
2. How does your peace with God affect you in the midst of suffering?
3. How can you, as a minister of this peace with God through our Lord Jesus Christ, help people who suffer the pains of justifying themselves to God without Christ's grace?

4. Can you remember a time when suffering produced endurance, endurance produced character and character produced a hope that did not disappoint because of God's love? Was this a personal experience?
5. Can you recall a situation when you wanted to suffer in order to take away someone's suffering for sin? Was this a form of works righteousness on your part? Were you trying to take on the role of Christ or just empathizing with the person's pain and anguish? What did you end up doing? How did you ask Jesus to help? How did you end up helping the person?
6. For your closing prayers, remember ways in which Jesus' one perfect sacrifice has been a consolation to you and people you know. Give thanks and praise to Our Lord for God's love being poured into our hearts through the Holy Spirit which has been given to us.

— 10 —
The Race for the Dead

Pitfall: You and the associate pastor compete against one another and divide the church.

And if a house is divided against itself, that house will not be able to stand.

Mark 3:25

Carl looked at Al and thought, "He's like a cow staring at a new gate."

This phrase of Luther's, spoken about an adversary, floated through the young pastor's mind as he looked at the old pastor sharpening pencil after pencil in the church office. The pencil sharpening had gone on for five minutes and created such a racket that the young pastor had to stop typing on the word processor.

Carl, the younger pastor, glared at Al, the elder pastor as Al trudged back to his desk. Al stared straight ahead.

As Carl-the-younger worked on the word processor, Al-the-elder scribbled away at plans for the church parking lot.

They hadn't spoken since The Race for the Dead two weeks ago. In just two weeks, the talk of their fight for power and control in the parish had taken on the air of a mythic saga, full of despairing love and lonely bitterness.

Actually, their fight was one of long, silent pouts and neglected paperwork. They were fighting like an old married couple with the deadly weapon of corrosive quiet and the pastoral administrative equivalents of dirty dishes, neglected garbage and an empty refrigerator. A battle of attrition. Who would break first?

The Race for the Dead occurred when a long-time member lay dying in the hospital. The pastors had decided to visit him individually on alternating days. The patient played the pastors against one another for maximum attention and sympathy.

One day, when Al-the-elder was visiting the man, the patient said that, "the other pastor, Carl-the-younger, never reads the Bible to me."

"I asked him why not, and Carl said that it was so mechanical to visit someone and read the Bible. Carl was more interested in reflecting my feelings back to me so I could deal with my impending death. That nearly killed me right there!"

On another day, when Carl-the-younger was visiting the man, the man said that Al-the-elder never listened to him, but just whipped out the Bible and cast incantations around him like a voodoo priest and left hurriedly. The dying man had asked Al why he didn't listen to him more when he visited.

Al-the-elder looked at his Bible. Al said after a while, "Let's say the Lord's Prayer," and rang the curtain down on the visit with the prayer's hurried recitation.

Relishing his role as a victim, the patient made each pastor feel that his life depended on that pastor's particular style. Though most people think hospital visits the most gloomy of pastoral duties, oddly it is one of the most uplifting for underappreciated clergy. They are rescuers, heroines and heroes with the good news for life and death. They really can't lose if they're careful and don't seem glib or insincere or callous.

Neither Al nor Carl were glib or insincere or callous. But they were competitive. Oh, one liked cars and would hear sermons against spending so much money getting from point A to point B.

One liked golf and would hear sermons against chasing a little white ball into holes and spending money on silly shoes.

Carl-the-younger looked at Al. Al looked like a carthorse when he walked; plodding, head down, seemingly no thoughts behind his big eyes.

Al-the-elder saw Carl looking at him. To Al, Carl seemed to be a hairless type of spider monkey. Leaping from one branch of the parish to the next, never too long in one place, cheery and noisy, but messy and untamed.

"What are *you* looking at?" Al asked.

"A guy going through the motions. Are you really here or did you check out of the pastorate when nobody was looking?"

"Listen," said Al-the-elder, "You just sit there surrounded by your computer and psychology books and think up stuff to do on Sunday with tamborines and toilet paper streamers, okay?"

"If you ever listened to people, you'd hear they like that stuff you call weird."

"Yeah, and if you ever cracked a book written by someone who wasn't committing some sort of sacriligious heresy in the name of trendy worship styles, you'd see the value in the old way."

"Oh sure," Carl-the-younger spouted, "Like how you really ministered to Ralph while he was dying; pounding him over the head with scripture, shoving the sacrament at him. You nearly drowned him in olive oil during the healing service you celebrated."

"Well, at least something was done for him."

"I was there for him; listening, reflecting, showing accurate empathy, vibrating intuitively with his resonance."

"Oh, for Pete's sake," the older pastor cried, "What are you, some sort of vibrating mattress for the "feel-good brigade?"

"He needed me and a listening ear more than he needed you and theology."

"He needed me and the Bible more than he needed you and your pop-psychology claptrap."

"Yeah, well whose hand was he holding when he died?"

"Yeah, well, whose office did the wife come to for comfort?"

"I can't help it if you got the only decent office in this dump!" Carl-the-younger yelled.

"I *knew* you always resented that I got first dibs on the office! I asked you what you wanted, but no; you play Saint Carl the essene. Not too much room or comfort for you."

"Your big butt needs the room and comfort more than mine. At least I exercise mine once and awhile!"

"Yeah," Al-the-elder shouted, "I noticed I can never find you when I need you. You're always jumping around like a damn monkey; branch to branch, never in one place. You do all your work but you go home early."

"What in the world is *that* supposed to mean?" Carl shouted back, "If I get my work done, I've earned the extra time to do with what I like. I can go where I please. I don't have to sit in this office, twiddling my thumbs behind a closed door like you; pretending I'm meditating or praying or something holy moly."

The two pastors are both out of breath. The secretary on the other side of the office has been forgotten until now. The secretary leans back in her chair and swivels it around to face the two pastors.

"You two jerks could both do with some of your own medicine. Al, read your Scripture about a house divided. Carl, try 'vibrating' with Al's 'resonating' with worry for all your new techniques and strategies, your youthful energy."

Both pastors were pouting again.

The secretary continued, "Then try one another's routine. Carl, you read more Scripture and learn from Al its power to comfort and sooth troubled hearts. Al, you listen more to Carl and other people. You can't just go through the rites and scripture as though its mere performance is enough, like a magic spell."

Both pastors pouted still.

"Look at you two poops! You're splitting up this parish. The flock has been startled and is looking for direction. People are nervous and worred about you two. Plans are falling apart. We're behind in some projects because you two are having communication trouble. More than one person has suggested marriage counseling for you both. And I don't mean with your spouses."

Carl looked at Al. He smiled, "Yeah, I suppose a divorce is out of the question."

Al looked at Carl over his glasses with a grin. "Yeah, we've got to think of the kids."

The secretary said, "You two might really think about some counseling. I hear a lot of worry and hurt, competition and jealousy in your voices. Remember, "the harvest is plentiful, but the laborers are few." Our Lord needs you here. We need you here. We need you both. I need you both."

It's nice how things work out sometimes. Al-the-elder learned to listen more and even conceded that liturgical dance was probably a tradition in church at least since the times the Psalms were written.

Carl learned the power of the Bible by memorizing parts of it so he didn't feel awkwardly clerical lugging it around on his daily routine. He saw the Scripture and rites of the church heal people in ways psychology couldn't.

The parish was happy again.

And the secretary, as you might have guessed, went on to seminary and eventually became Carl and Al's bishop.

Study and Reflection Guides For:
The Race for the Dead

The Pastoral Pitfall: You and the associate pastor compete against one another and divide the church.

A Pastor's Insight: "What splendid people have fallen! No doubt all of them were overcome by the wretched subtle danger of becoming secure, so that they thought: We are now close to God; there is no danger; we know God; we have done this and that. They did not see how they made themselves the first before God . . . That is why I dare say it is necessary for this gospel to be preached to those in our day who know the Gospel, to me and others like me, who are able to teach and train all the world and consider ourselves very close to God, as having consumed God's Spirit completely, with feathers and bones . . . For these words strike at what lies deepest in the heart of a man: his spiritual conceit."

Martin Luther

Questions About the Story

1. Why are the pastors competitive?
2. How do they show their competitiveness; in their thoughts, words and deeds?
3. Why do you think they are so competitive?
4. How do you think this competition will hurt the church? How did the patient benefit from it?
5. How did the secretary minister to each of the pastor's separate views of ministry?

Questions About Your Ministry

1. Have you ever been in a team ministry?
2. Were you ever competitive? Was your associate?
3. How can competitiveness be good in a team ministry?
4. How can it disrupt the ministry?
5. How do you address this competition? Do you ever really mention it?
6. Would a third person, not connected with your ministry, help your team deal with this disruptive force?
7. Would the intervention of your bishop's office or clergy cluster help or hinder? Why?

Questions About You

1. How do you pace your day's work?
2. How do you know you're doing enough?
3. Do you work too hard? Do you plan your day?
4. Do you look to other pastors and their schedules for perspective on their busyness or effectiveness?
5. When do you feel competitive in your pastoral or social life? Envious? Jealous?
6. When do you feel competitive in your professional life? Envious? Jealous?
7. To whom do you express these powerful emotions?

How Can Your Group Support You?

1. Let the group tell you what they admire about your professional skills, your pastoral personality, your administrative skills, other personal qualities.
2. Ask for help in areas where you feel competitive or weak.
3. Does your group have some techniques for addressing professional competition problems? Try role-playing.

4. What would you change in your ministry if you had the power to do so? Ask the group to help you plan for your hopes to come true. Ask for suggestions, prayer and proven solutions.

Meditation and Prayer Focus
Hebrews 12:1-2

1. A race is competitive. And, it seems, Paul calls us to race together as a team. What weight or sin can you lay aside to persevere with your team in the Christian race? Can your group help you lay aside this weight?
2. How does a cloud of witnesses help you get strength for this competition?
3. Who are these witnesses? Are they with you in your group? Can they help you to lay aside every weight and sin which clings so closely?
4. A competitive nature might prohibit you from admitting you are competitive in the first place! How will you lay aside this first weight? Will looking at Jesus and his endurance help as you despise this shame? (v. 2)
5. Pray for specific weights to be lifted from you.

www.ingramcontent.com/pod-product-compliance
Lightning Source LLC
Chambersburg PA
CBHW060848050426
42453CB00008B/898